Ainsty Bounds Walk

By the same author:

DALES TRAVERSE

Ainsty Bounds Walk

A 44-mile circular route in the Vale of York

by
Simon Townson

Dalesman Books
1984

The Dalesman Publishing Company Ltd.,
Clapham, via Lancaster LA2 8EB

First published 1984

ISBN: 0 85206 790 9

Printed by Alf Smith & Co., Bradford.

Contents

Cover photograph of walkers between Boston Spa and Wetherby by Robert Rixon.

Maps by Hazel Chester and Janet Acland (page 42).

Drawings in the text by Frank Armstrong, Stanley Bond, B. Cudworth, Robert Lawson and D. C. Smith.

Preface

SHOULD you be a walker whose sole aim is to get from A to B then you only need to be told that this book describes in some detail a walk 44 miles in length, on which there is no climbing of significance, and which joins the end (or beginning whichever way you look at it) of the Ainsty Bounds with a link of the Ebor Way. You can now collect your equipment, maps, etc, together, plan your route and complete the walk in two days or at your own leisure.

For some whose interest lies, however, not only in the ultimate achievement of completion of a long-distance walk, but also in the beauty of the countryside, its history and inhabitants, this walk has much more to offer. Should I meet you somewhere along the way, we'll have a pint at the village pub, look around the ancient church, or perhaps you can tell me of the odd thousand or two things I've almost certainly missed along the walk.

The idea for this long-distance path, virtually all of it covered by rights-of-way, originated in 1975 from the West Riding Area of the Ramblers' Association. Whilst there are no spectacular or superbly breath-taking views, the way passes through delightful countryside, steeped in history, and where the walker can be assured a friendly welcome from the inhabitants. Unfortunately there are no badges or certificates for this walk, but I hope it will not stop you from doing the Ainsty Bounds.

Finally, may I place on record my appreciation of all the assistance given by so many people in the preparation of this book and particularly members of the West Riding Area of the Ramblers' Association.

To all those walkers about to set out on the walk, may I say "good luck". I hope that you enjoy the walk as much as I did.

S. Townson
18 Victoria Street
Wetherby
West Yorkshire
LS22 4RE

Introduction

The Walk

The Ainsty Bounds is approximately 44 miles in length and, except for about eight miles of road, is entirely over public rights-of-way. Fortunately most of the roads are pleasant country lanes with very little traffic and with ample grass verges to walk along. On the debit side there are a few problems at present, particularly between Cattle, Moor Monkton, Acaster Selby and Bolton Percy. These are however just minor irritations on a walk which is relatively easy to follow and which for the most part uses the paths and tracks trod by our ancestors to pass from one farmstead to another or one village to another and which in some instances even now are the only link between the farms and villages.

The Way passes through or alongside quite a lot of areas of woodland which provide the walker with many opportunities to study the great variety of plant and animal life and, although the highest point is only some one hundred feet, the walker will find that almost every route provides remarkable views over the Vale of York and the immediate countryside. Whilst the main objective has been to provide a long-distance walk from Tadcaster to Tadcaster through the ancient city of York, every opportunity has been taken to visit places of interest, passing along ancient roads wherever possible.

Whilst the paths are almost exclusively over established rights-of-way, it must be appreciated that the walker is only entitled to walk the path and that in this type of countryside it is absolutely essential that the farmer's rights should also be recognised. Walkers should always walk in single file through growing crops, and don't forget that this includes meadow land — hay is a valuable crop which can be destroyed by a herd of ramblers charging across the fields. If damage does occur to fences, please don't leave them in a state where animals can stray; make a temporary repair and call on the nearest farmer and tell him. This may take a little courage but if the walking community expects to be understood it must in turn respect the interest of the farmer. Dogs should if at all possible be left at home

but, if this is not practicable, should be kept on a lead at all times. In the lambing season the sheep will become restless even if they only scent the dog, with possible harm to lambs and/or sheep — during lambing leave the dog at home! Finally, read the Country Code and do your best to see that not only yourself but other walkers along the way obey it.

The sections described happen to be convenient for bus services but they can be varied according to the requirements of the individual and the time available. This is a walk to take your time over; a good idea would be to spend several weekends which would provide ample opportunities to look more closely at the villages, have a chat with the locals and visit the churches.

Accommodation

The Youth Hostel to stay at is York:
Haverford, Water End, Clifton, York YO3 6LT.

Camp sites are practically non-existent but most farmers will allow you to pitch a tent for the night. The one council-owned site at York is unfortunately only open during the summer months, but is very conveniently sited on the riverside and it is actually on the walk.

The other accommodation that can be found is in the Ramblers' Association Bed and Breakfast Guide which can be purchased from any bookshop.

Finding the way

The directions given are fairly detailed but no one should set out on the walk armed only with this book. Words can be quite deceptive at times and quite small changes in the face of the countryside can result in vastly different interpretation of the written word. It is essential therefore to invest in at least a set of 1:50,000 Ordnance Survey maps but, if you can possibly afford it, obtain a set of 1:25,000; they will make route finding so much easier. Read the directions given, mark up your route prior to setting out and then use your maps, resorting to the book only when problems arise or you have a few minutes available to refresh your memory. The way is over fairly easy paths but this should not be used as an excuse to be badly equipped. Always make sure that you carry a compass, are well equipped with spare clothing and waterproofs and carry sufficient food — chocolate, nuts, etc. — to last 24 hours.

Maps required

1:50,000 First Series: 105 York
1:25,000 Second Series: SE44/54 Tadcaster

HEALAUGH, NEAR TADCASTER.

The Route of Ainsty Bounds

The Route of Ainsty Bounds

Tadcaster to Wetherby

Take the footpath, signposted 'Newton Kyme', at the Leeds end of the bridge, by the side of the River Wharfe, upstream past the churchyard and weir. Keep along the riverside until you get fairly close to Newton Kyme church, where you leave the river and pass the entrance to the churchyard. The path to the road goes in front of the garden to Newton Kyme Hall, associated with the Fairfax family from the seventeenth century.

Keep forward along the minor road (see map), ignoring side turnings, to the Otley-Tadcaster turnpike where turn right for 200 yards to reach the Rudgate crossing. The bridleway on the right here takes you to the site of the Roman St. Helen's ford and fort.

Along the riverside take care using the anglers' high level path (not on the Definitive Map) beyond the old railway bridge which leads to the very attractive wooded riverside right-of-way to Boston Spa passing the Spa Baths building.

Boston Spa

After going along the riverside path to look at the weir, return and cross over the narrow Thorp Arch bridge, and keep straight ahead passing the Pax Inn and village school and after about half-a-mile turn left along a green track. This soon turns right and winds along to Flint Mill Grange, where it is sign-posted to Wetherby — a side track here continues to the Flint Mill, a dead end.

Past the Grange the farm track turns right, but the path continues straight forward along the edge of woodland (see Wetherby map) towards Wetherby. If you do not wish to go into Wetherby itself, make for the racecourse direct as shown on the map.

WALTON, NEAR WETHERBY.

Wetherby to Moor Monkton

After deciding not to go into Wetherby, continue from the racecourse and turn left down B1224 for a short distance till you come to Ingmanthorpe Hall entrance. Continue along the drive past the hall till you come to a fork with a farm track to the right. Take farm track past farm and continue towards Bickerton (map: Ainsty Bridge Route) and on to Lingcroft Farm. After reaching Lingcroft Farm go into the farmyard; there is a wooden gate at the back of the farm buildings where you will find a line of telegraph poles — follow them to Moorside Farm. Follow the farm track to Tockwith Broad Oak till you come to the main road which goes to Cowthorpe. Turn right, then turn left at the crossroads towards Cattal.

Follow the main road to Cattal till you see Cattal Lodge on your right — do not go into Cattal Lodge drive. Continue along the road for a short while till you see a footpath (sign) which goes into a field of crops. Keep along the hedge side on your left and follow it along till you come to the corner of the field. Here you will find a stile which goes onto a track; turn left, and continue along this until you come to some farm buildings. Go through the gate by the farm buildings straight to the far corner where you will find another gate — go through that and you will come to a beck. Follow the beck to the right through another gate and look out for high banking which is the River Nidd. **Take care not to get lost on this section as there are no footpath signs.**

Continue along the River Nidd to Skewkirt Hall (follow map) and Skip Bridge. After approaching the A59 road from Wilstrop Hall turn right for a short distance along the main road. The footpath continues between two buildings (see 'Beware of the Dog' notice — it's usually chained up). One of these buildings was a drovers' inn — Skip Bridge probably derives from Sheep Bridge. Through the farmyard keep forward along the hedge-side track to a gate, where go through and turn right. Follow the hedge for several fields, passing a black barn, until you reach a stile and bridge to the track on the other side. Keep forward parallel to the river, which re-appears on your left

The track goes through a succession of gates and becomes a double-hedged lane before reaching a road, where turn left and then right to the single street of Moor Monkton village.

GUILDHALL, YORK.

Moor Monkton to York

At the far end, where the road turns right, go through a gate and follow a track parallel to the river. Avoid bearing right, away from the river, but keep forward and through a small gate to the confluence of the Nidd and Ouse. Follow the riverside path (now along the Ouse of course) through to Nether Poppleton, soon passing Red House where there is an old chapel.

Unfortunately the ferry to the riverside path on the opposite bank no longer operates. From the 'Pile of Stones' War memorial on the small green, turn left along the road. (For Upper Poppleton Green, the Maypole and the station, take a signposted footpath to the right, just along the road). At a road junction turn left past Manor Farm to the church (note the gallery inside). Turn back a few yards from the churchyard and take a signposted path ('Millfield Lane') through a gate at the bend in the road. Turn left at the end (Signposted 'Parish Church') and walk down the main road where you turn left to the traffic lights, passing the Ainsty Inn. Continue along the road until you come to traffic lights. Turn left to Clifton over the rialway bridge; if you look to the left you will see the River Ouse in all its glory. Continue on to Water End Bridge, Clifton, the start of the walk through the ancient city of York. Here you can follow the short route on the map; this is a good chance for an overnight stop at the Youth Hostel or a bed and breakfast place.

York to Bishopthorpe

After leaving the Youth Hostel or overnight stop for bed and breakfast, make your way to the bridge at Water End, Clifton. Walk along the River Ouse (left-side) for a short way till you reach the railway bridge on your right. You can see the Railway Museum which is worth a visit, but if you don't have the time continue along till you have gone under the bridge. You will see a flight of steps on your left; go up the steps on to the footbridge which goes alongside the railway bridge.

Cross over to the other side and continue along the river to Lendal Bridge — the Museum Gardens are on your left. When you have reached the bridge go under it and go along North Street. (If you don't want to do this, and would prefer to have a look at some gardens, there is a path through them which goes to Ouse Bridge.) Turn left onto Ouse Bridge and go over to the other side. You will find some steps leading down to the river at this point; you will go past the King's Arms (see special note below). Continue along the river and you will pass Cliffords Tower and the Castle Museum. Go up the steps to Skeldergate Bridge (which dates back to 1881). Cross over to the other side of the bridge to go down to the river and follow the road alongside. A little further along you will find the only camping.

Keep to the riverside, passing the baths and a very pleasant park on your right, until the road turns away to the right and your path continues along the river bank. For the next two miles there are no problems — a very pleasant riverside walk with a well defined path and adequate stiles eventually goes under the new bridge serving York by-pass and continues to Bishopthorpe Palace, the home of the Archbishop of York. A lane leads between the crematorium and the Palace grounds — if you're very quiet you may see some grey squirrels. At the end of the lane turn left along the road passing the entrance to the Palace, the well-preserved remains of the former village church being down the lane to the left.

Special Note: Take extreme care during flooding, the walk along the Ouse between bridges floods very badly. A very interesting building which gets flooded is the King's Arms, dating back to the 15th century. If you get chance to have a drink take note of the chart on the wall which shows the flooding depths.

Bishopthorpe to Tadcaster

After you have reached the ruins of the former village church, take notice of the danger sign and keep away from the arch. At the back of the cross near the river keep to your right and go onto the path through the clump of trees. Follow the path which goes along the river side. You will now see a splendid view of river boats. On this section of the walk you will encounter a few stiles till you reach the railway swing birdge. Take note of the footpath sign which tells you to go under it; do not wonder off this section of the path as it is **private property.**

Continue along the river till you reach the track which leads into Acaster Malbis. Once you have reached Acaster you will note that there is a pub which serves light refreshments and food (you will need to refresh for the rest of the walk). Continue left along the road and follow the road which goes past the post office and caravan site. Continue along the road for about 50 yards and you will come to a car park which leads to the river. Go through the car park and you will find a gate on your right-hand side and the footpath sign. Go through the gate and continue along the path (do not forget to lock gate after you have come through) till you reach another gate (please close).

When you are nearing Acaster Selby you will see a hedge with a stile in it and a small bridge. Cross over both and walk towards the fence; climb over the stile and be careful where you walk as this is a well kept lawn. Walk towards the road, turn right and continue along till you come to the main road which goes to Appleton Roebuck. Turn left and continue along this for about 1½ miles. If you wish to do the alternative route see map; if not, continue along the road which goes into the village. You have two choices of light refreshment but only one for a meal. The pub which you go past to Bolton Percy has light refreshments; the other one is the Shoulder of Mutton which is on the village green past the school and church.

Continue past the public house on the road which goes to Tadcaster and keep along the road for a short distance until you see a footpath sign. Turn left down the street till you come to Church Lane which is on your right. Follow Church Lane which now goes to Bolton Percy but take extra care as you will encounter a new railway that has been built and there have been a lot of construction works going on. Continue along the lane until you meet a road. Turn left then turn right, go along the road for a short distance and then turn left to pass

the church which is very interesting and worth a look at inside. (Please refer to Places of Interest — Bolton Percy). Here again you have an alternative route (see map). You will see a footpath sign at the corner of the wall of the church grounds near the turning to the right towards the inn. If you do not wish to go to the inn continue down the road past the row of houses and you will see a wicker gate which leads to the high footbridge (or you can go through the car park). Please keep to the left-hand side of the big cage that dogs are kept in; do not wander around the inn grounds unless you are going to have a meal and a drink.

Proceed along the footbridge and onto the footpath which leads into a field. Keep to the left and follow the hedge round the field till you come to a gate onto a farm track. Turn right and you will notice a footpath sign which says Ulleskelf ferry — I am sorry to say that this ferry does not exist any more. Proceed along the track till you reach a gate which has a sign on it and says 'Bolton Lodge'. Follow this track through until you come to a bend where you will see a very faint track which leads alongside a field towards a wood. After reaching the wood, go through the gate on your left and immediately turn right and follow the fence round until you come to the railway embankment and reach the river. You will now have to scramble over a wooden fence to go under the railway bridge and follow the river all the way to Tadcaster.

Maps of the Route

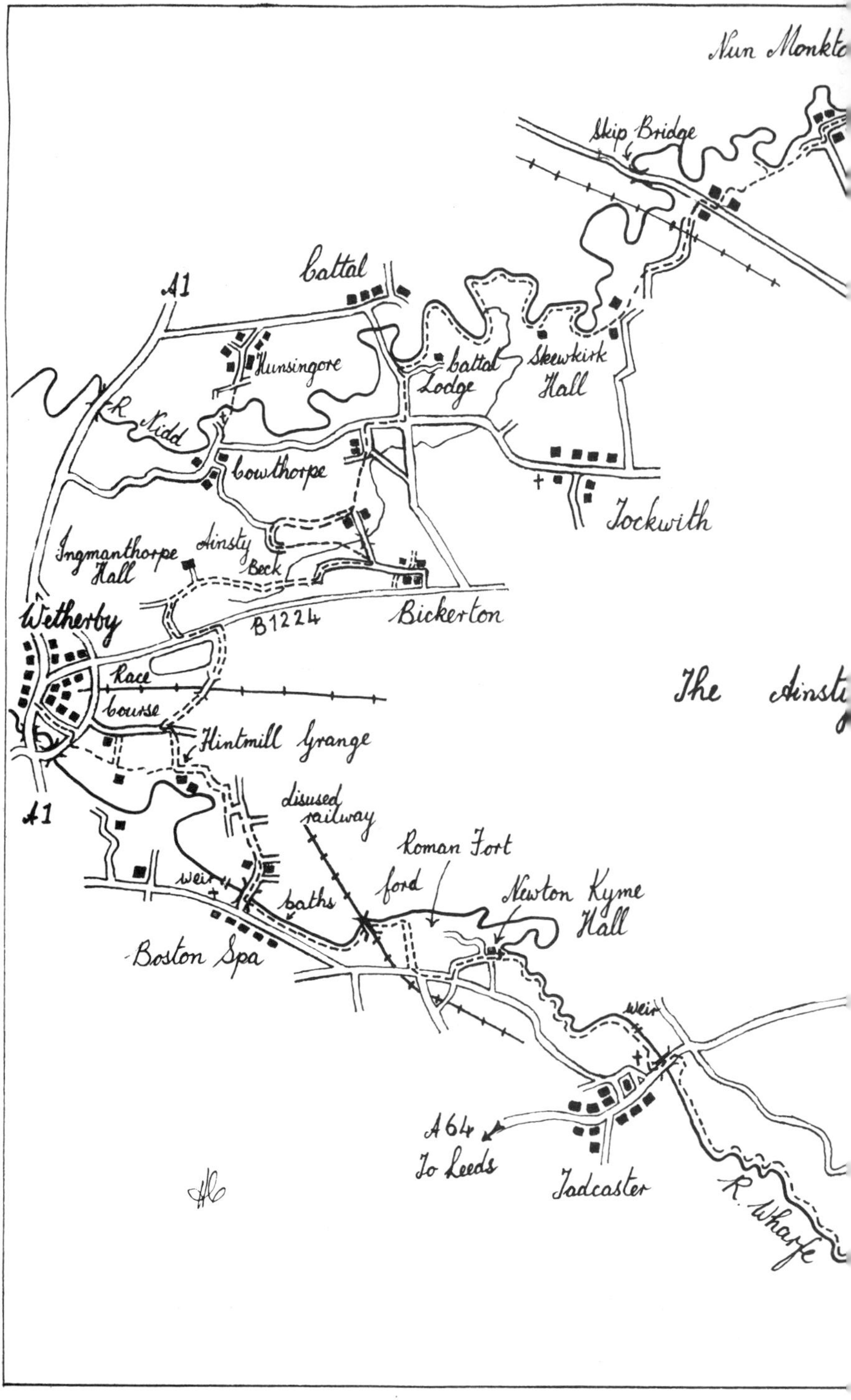

Nun Monkto
Skip Bridge
Cattal
A1
Hunsingore
R. Nidd
Cattal Lodge
Skewkirk Hall
Cowthorpe
Tockwith
Ingmanthorpe Hall
Ainsty Beck
Wetherby
B1224
Bickerton
Race course
The Ainsty
Hintmill Grange
A1
disused railway
Roman Fort
ford
weir
baths
Newton Kyme Hall
Boston Spa
weir
A64 To Leeds
Tadcaster
R. Wharfe

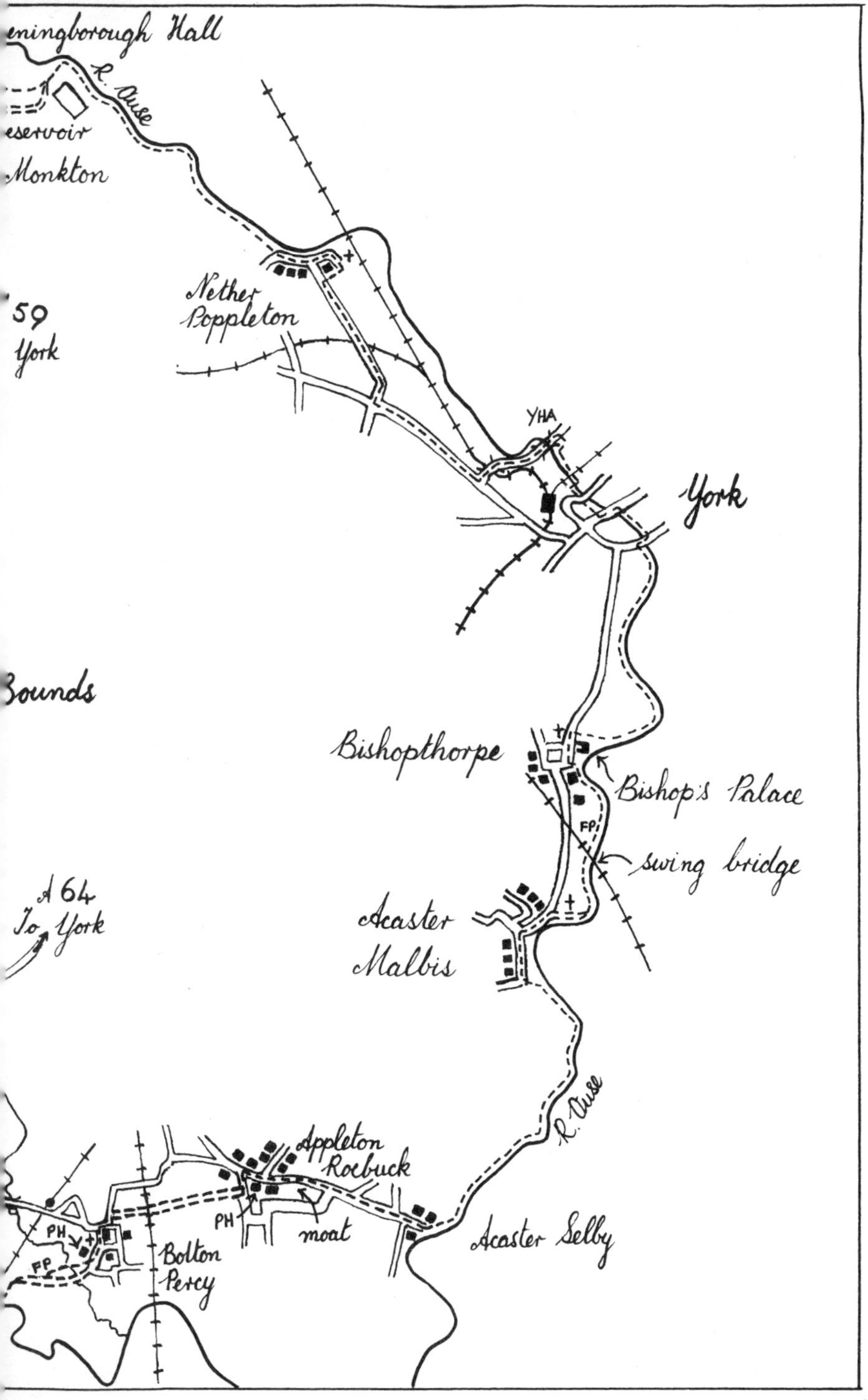

eningborough Hall
R. Ouse
eservoir
Monkton
59
York
Nether Poppleton
YHA
York
Bounds
Bishopthorpe
Bishop's Palace
FP
swing bridge
Acaster Malbis
A 64
To York
R. Ouse
Appleton Roebuck
PH
moat
Acaster Selby
PH
Bolton Percy
FP

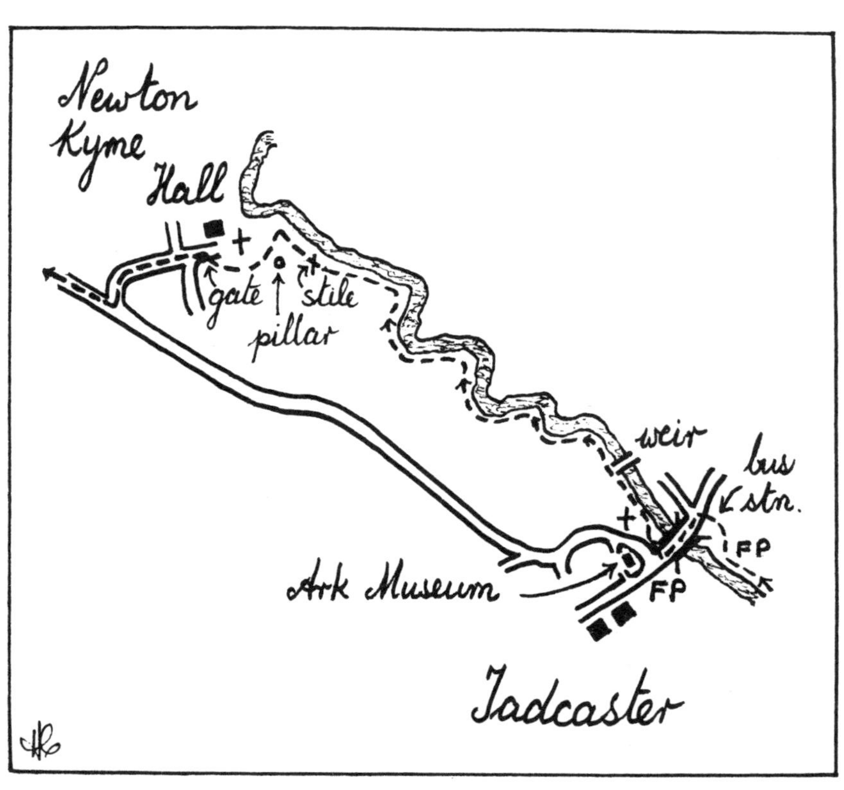
Newton
Kyme
Hall
gate
stile
pillar
weir
bus
stn.
FP
FP
Ark Museum
Tadcaster

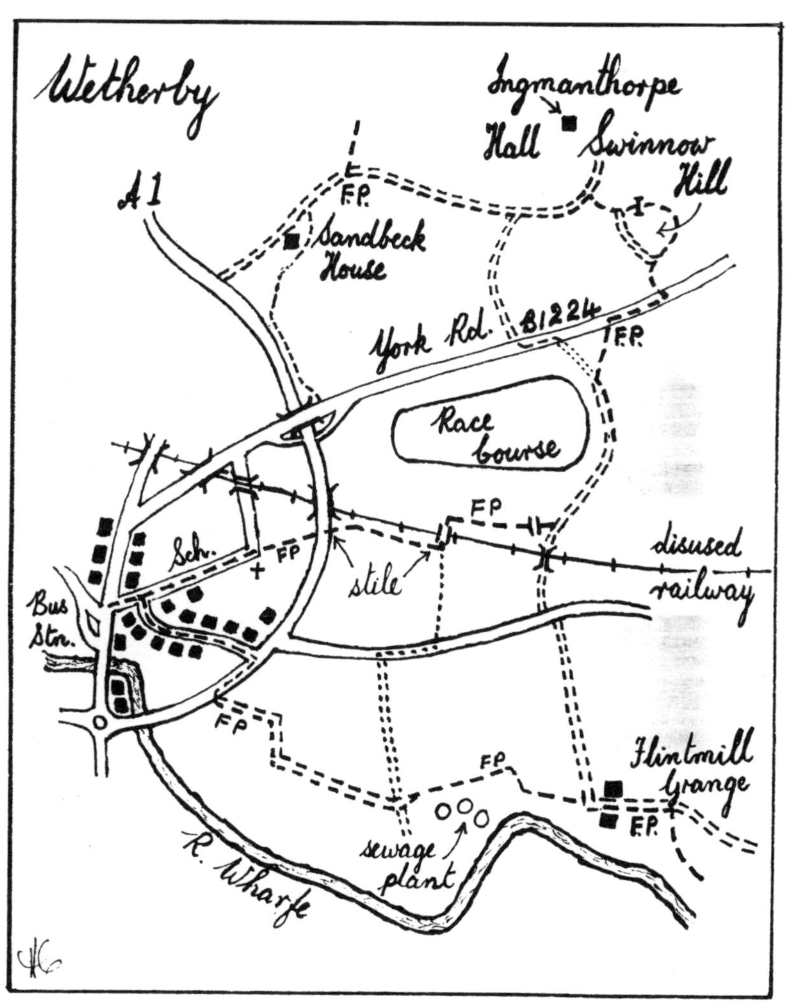
Wetherby
Ingmanthorpe
Hall
Swinnow
Hill
A1
F.P.
Sandbeck
House
York Rd.
B1224
F.P.
Race
course
F.P.
Sch.
F.P.
stile
disused
railway
Bus
Stn.
F.P.
F.P.
Flintmill
Grange
F.P.
sewage
plant
R. Wharfe

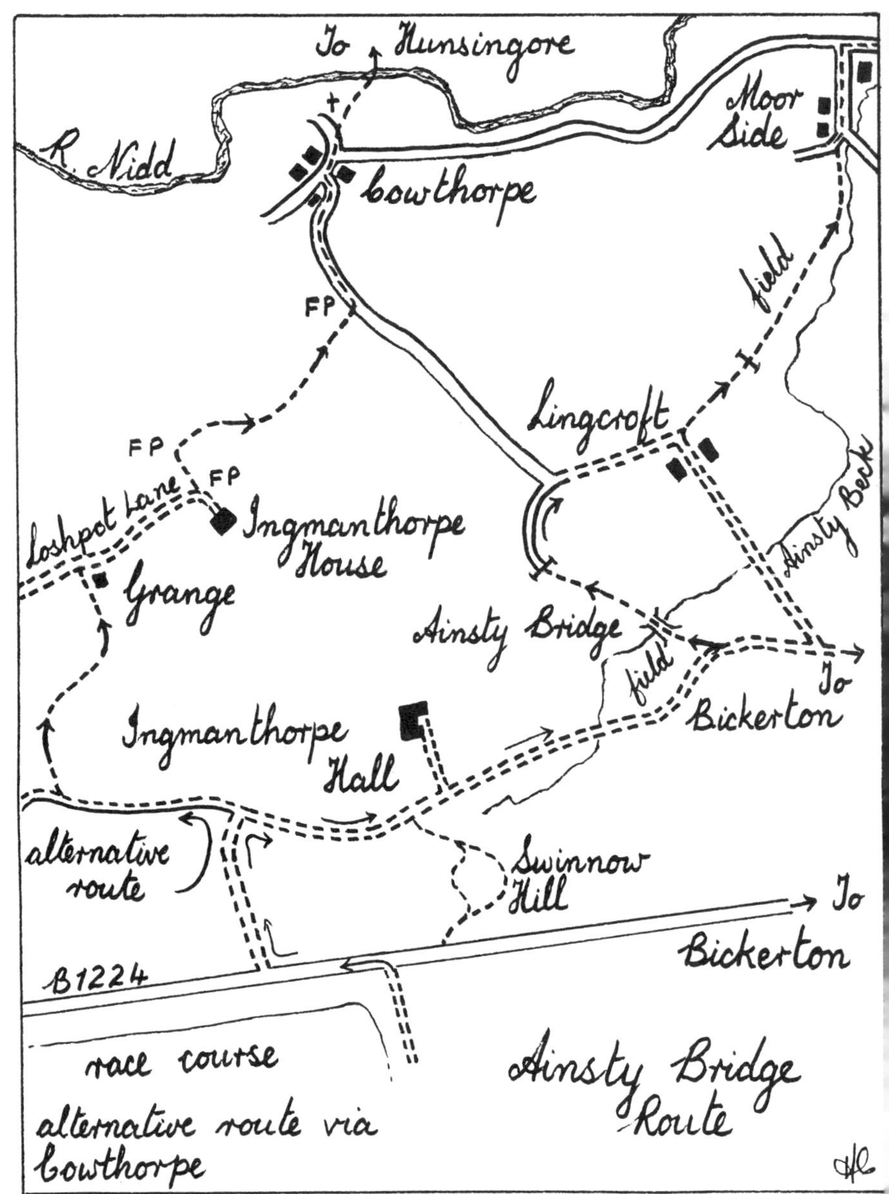
To Hunsingore
R. Nidd
Cowthorpe
Moor Side
FP
field
Lingcroft
FP
FP
Loshpot Lane
Ingmanthorpe House
Grange
Ainsty Beck
Ainsty Bridge
field
To Bickerton
Ingmanthorpe Hall
alternative route
Swinnow Hill
To Bickerton
B1224
race course
Ainsty Bridge Route
alternative route via Cowthorpe

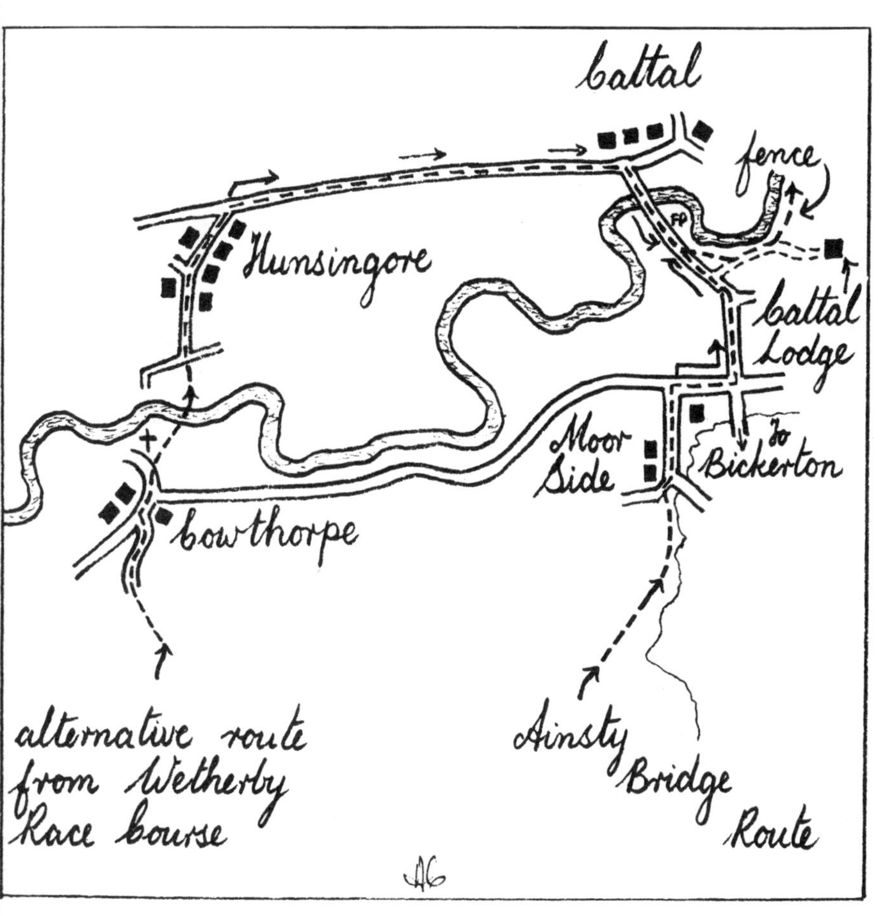
Cattal
fence
Hunsingore
FP
Cattal
Lodge
Moor
Side
To
Bickerton
Cowthorpe
alternative route
from Wetherby
Race Course
Ainsty
Bridge
Route
AG

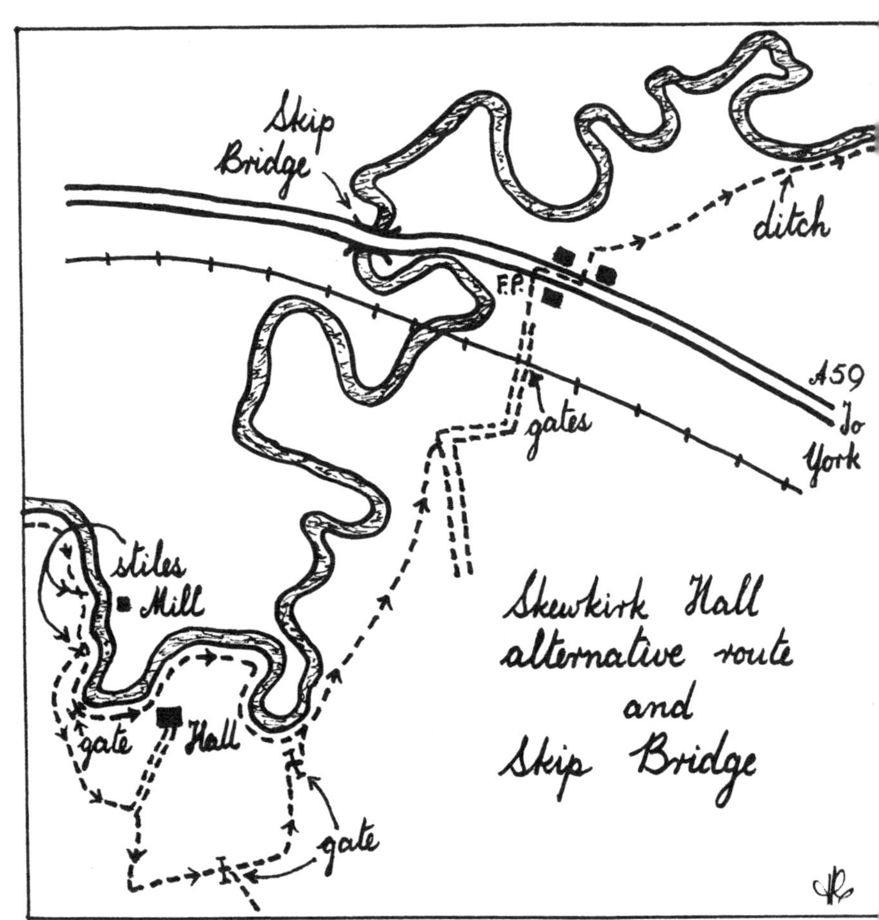
Skip Bridge
ditch
F.P.
A59
To York
gates
stiles
Mill
Skewkirk Hall alternative route and Skip Bridge
gate
Hall
gate

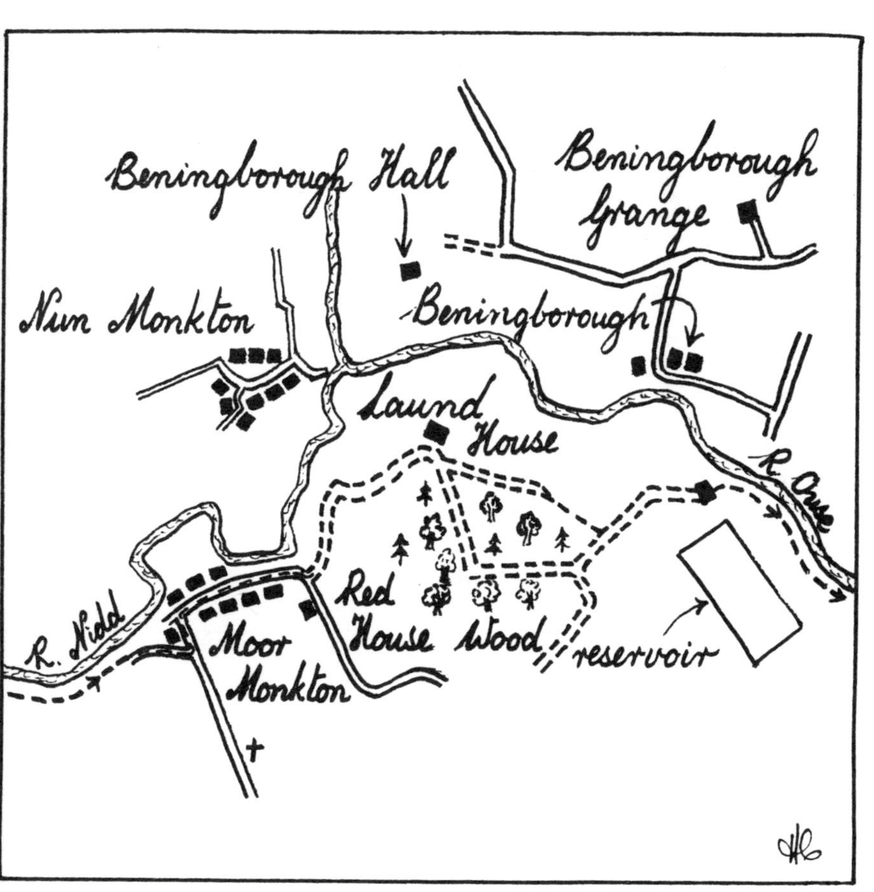
Beningborough Hall
Beningborough Grange
Nun Monkton
Beningborough
Laund House
R. Ouse
R. Nidd
Red House Wood
reservoir
Moor Monkton

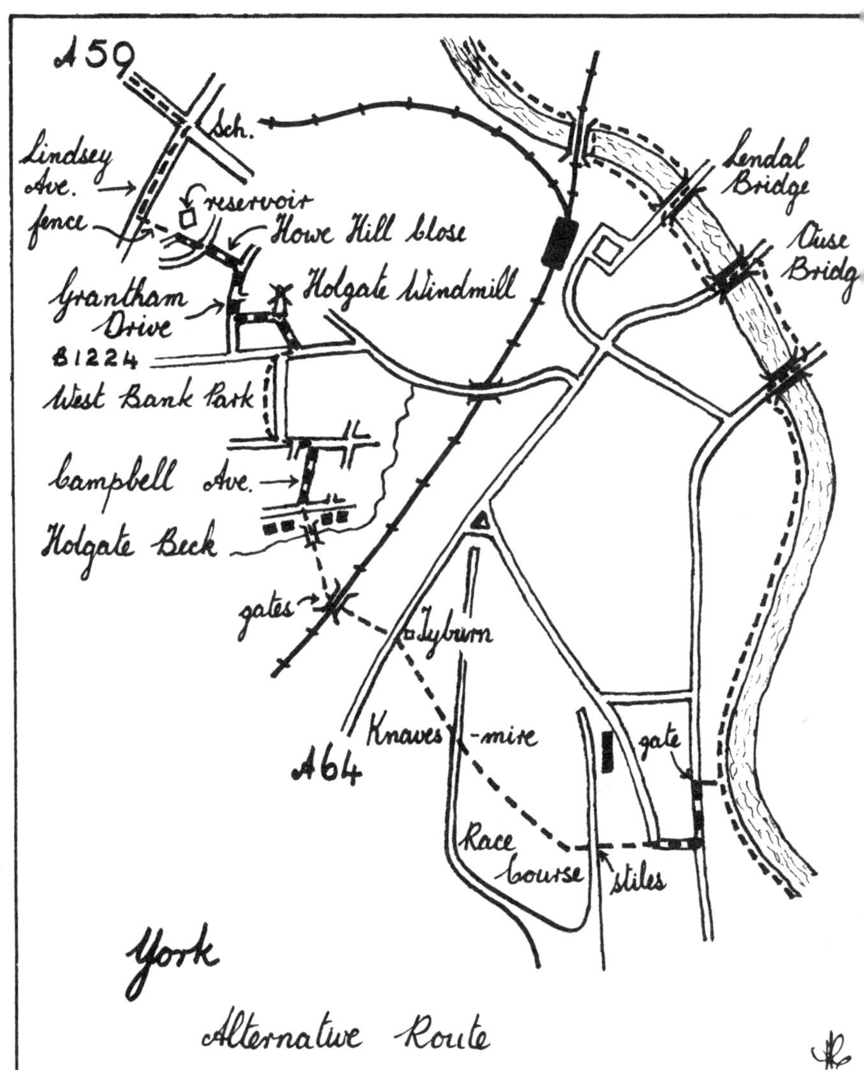
A59
Sch.
Lindsey Ave.
fence
reservoir
Howe Hill Close
Grantham Drive
Holgate Windmill
B1224
West Bank Park
Campbell Ave.
Holgate Beck
gates
Tyburn
Knaves-mire
A64
Race Course
stiles
gate
Lendal Bridge
Ouse Bridg
York
Alternative Route

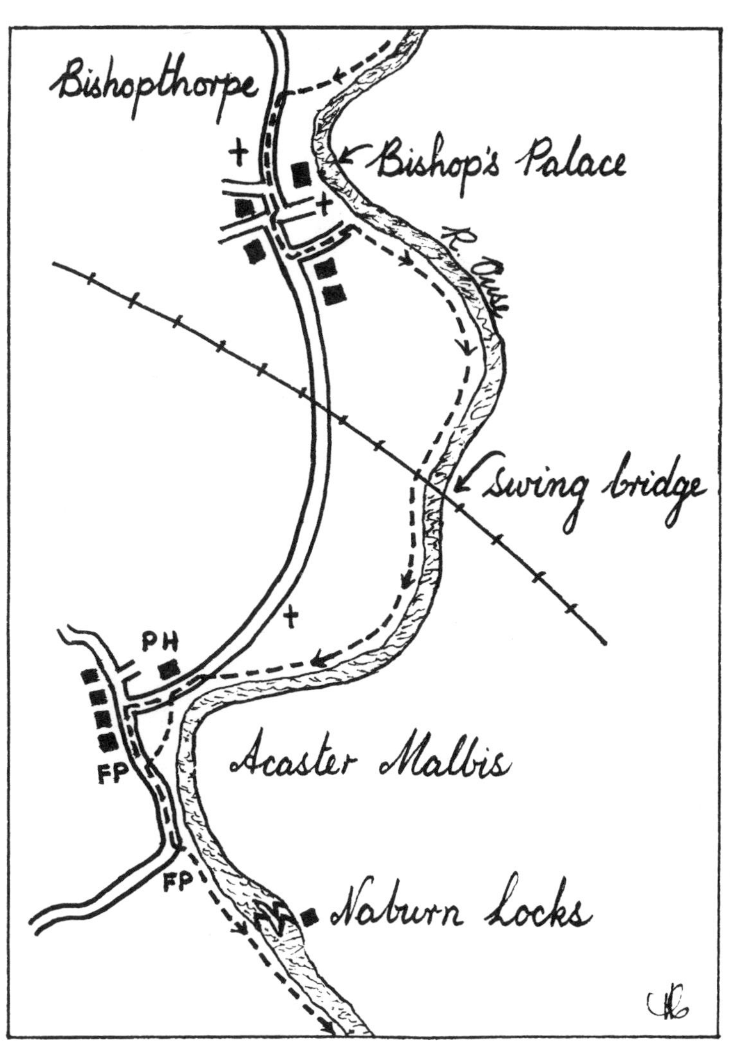
Bishopthorpe
Bishop's Palace
R. Ouse
Swing bridge
PH
FP
Acaster Malbis
FP
Naburn Locks

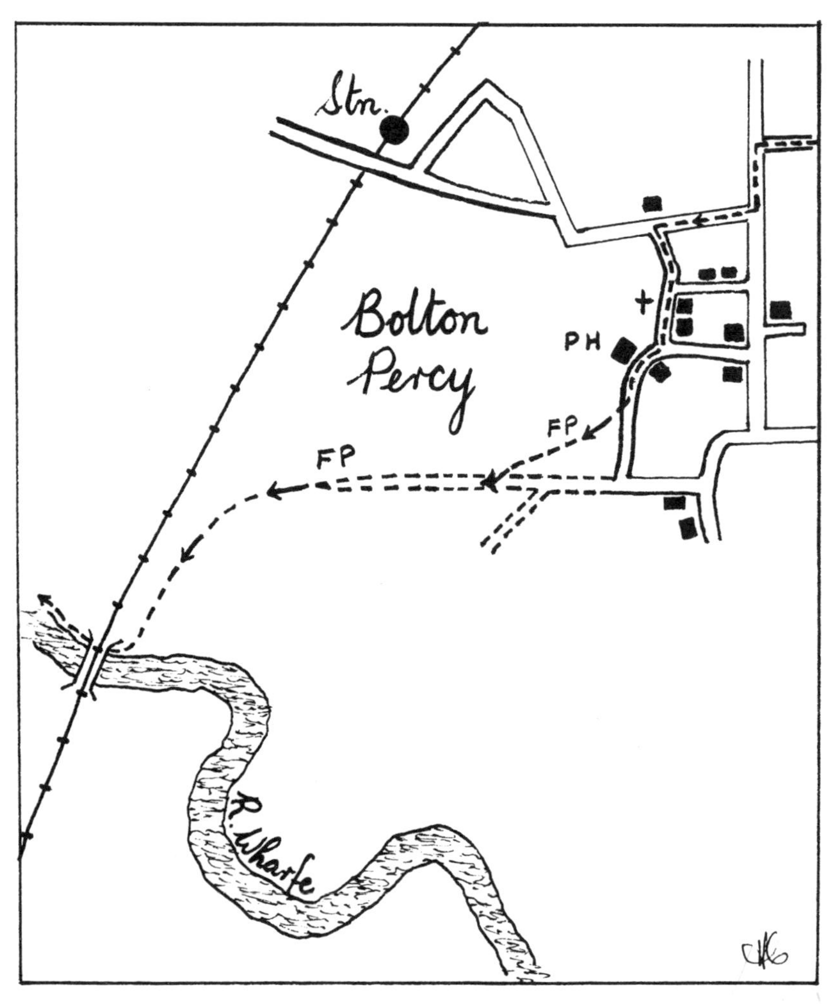
Stn.
Bolton Percy
PH
FP
FP
R. Wharfe

Places of Interest

Places of Interest

Tadcaster

The town has been brewing beer since the 18th century and the breweries are the most conspicuous objects in its landscape today. St. Mary's church has traces of Norman work inside, but it is mainly Perpendicular, a fine white stone building which was taken down between 1875 and 1877 and reconstructed 5ft. higher up to protect it from River Wharfe floods. Its exterior is enlivened by pinnacles and gargoyles. It has fine modern woodwork. The Wharfe bridge is early 18th century, later widened, with seven arches. Above it stands the viaduct constructed in 1849 but the railway that should have used it was never built. Tadcaster, a Roman outpost for York, was known then as Calcaria. The Ark Museum, built near the church in the 15th century and used as a meeting place by Dissenters in the 17th century, is maintained by a brewery and open at advertised times. Tadcaster is two miles north of Towton, a hamlet near which a bloody battle of the Wars of the Roses was fought in a snowstorm on 29 March 1461. A cross near the road to Saxton marks the field where 50,000 men fought — said to be the largest number ever engaged on English soil — and thousands died.

Boston Spa

A large village famous for its river fishing and Spa Baths and also for its beautiful mill which stands by the weir.

Wetherby

This town stands on an angle or bend of the Wharfe named by the early Saxons "Wederbi". The bridge is a handsome structure build in 1823-4 and for some years was considered the finest in Yorkshire. The old bridge, portions of which still remain built into the new, was erected from the ruins of the castle which in ancient days stood on a commanding site near to and facing up the vale to the west. The site is still known as Castle Garth. Up to 1824 the whole of the town with the Manor of Wetherby was owned by the Duke of Devonshire who effected a great many improvements in the place. It was then sold by

PRIORY FARM, NEAR TADCASTER.

public auction in 174 lots. The manorial rights, including market tolls, etc, were purchased by Mr. Wilson of Wetherby Grange and were subsequently inherited by his nephew, Andrew Fountayne Wilson Montague of Ingmanthorpe Hall.

Wetherby is well known for its racecourse and is famous for its steeplechases which are held annually on Easter Monday and Tuesday.

In the 13th century a chapel reputedly stood on Wetherby Bridge; little is known but it was dedicated to St. Mary. It is very probable that the bridge chapel was destroyed in 1548 and another place of worship was erected in the market place in 1755. The old chapel had a very low thatched roof and was a primitive-looking structure placed in orthodox fashion east and west with the entrance at the west end. The new chapel built soon after was on a site near to where the old one stood. This building continued to serve until 1841 when it was removed to make way for the Town Hall and the Court House. The present St. James's was built in 1840-1.

Wetherby has become a busy town with very fine buildings. The

Town Hall is one of them and has a market round it every Thursday and a very old cattle market every Monday.

Ingmanthorpe Hall

The Hall dates back to the 1820s and was once owned by Andrew Fountayne Wilson Montague. At one time it stood on a different site, possibly on the corner of the bend near the entrance to the drive.

Newton Kyme

A village which is full of history, some dating back to the 12th century, is worth a moment of your time to look around — an imposing Hall, the remains of the castle, and a church which is in beautiful surroundings. The approach from the Boston Spa to Tadcaster road speaks for itself with the splendid row of lime trees, some of which were planted by Admiral Robert Fairfax whose family owned the Hall in 1725.

The Parish includes the hamlets of Newton Kyme and Toulston, the small housing estate connected with the Papyrus paper mill, and Tadcaster Grammar School. It is mentioned in the Domesday Survey though there is no reference to a church. It is likely that there was an early Roman Settlement to the west of the present village, near St. Helen's ford across the River Wharfe, and "Newton" refers to the new enclosure and village on slightly higher ground, where there

would be less danger of flooding. "Kyme" was probably added in the 13th century when the family of Kymbe or Kyme held the manor.

The oldest part of the church is probably twelfth century, and it is likely that double pillars (twin-shafted responds) near the font and similar ones between the chancel and chapel date from that time. The main structure, including the nave, chancel, chapel and base of the tower, is probably thirteenth century, though not necessarily planned as a whole or built at the same time within the century. The sedilia (seats in the wall near the altar) and the piscina (a bowl in the wall with an outlet pipe to earth), together with the priest's door in the chancel, are also thought to be thirteenth century. The font is thought to date from the twelfth century, though the base is modern. The brass eagle lectern was presented in 1899 and the old sanctuary chairs in 1935. The two-manual organ, by M. Sagar of Leeds, was moved from the west gallery to its present position in 1893-4. It was completed overhauled and restored in 1976.

York

The fascinating townscape of this walled city illustrates much of its nearly 2,000 years of history. Although York possesses in its Minster the largest medieval church in northern Europe, the general scale of its buildings is small and human.

York has been a garrison town ever since Roman times — it is now the headquarters of Northern Command. For the sightseer, a multi-angular tower remains from Roman York, the west corner of the Roman fortress. The inside of this fine ruin can be seen beside the City Library (and Information Centre) in Museum Street and the outside from Museum Gardens.

Medieval York is everywhere, not least in the web of narrow streets. The Shambles and Stonegate are two of the best preserved examples. But the Minster is the city's chief glory, appropriate to the dignity of an archbishopric. Built between 1220 and 1470 and at least the fourth church on that site, it is a textbook of Early English, Decorated and Perpendicular styles.

In the Middle Ages, York was England's second city, a great religious and commercial centre, fattening on the wool trade. The economic impact of the Dissolution was cushioned by the establishment here of the Council of the North. When this was abolished in the 17th century, York declined. It revived in the 18th century as a social centre for county families. The racecourse on the

ST. WILLIAM'S COLLEGE, YORK.

ST. MARY'S ABBEY, YORK.

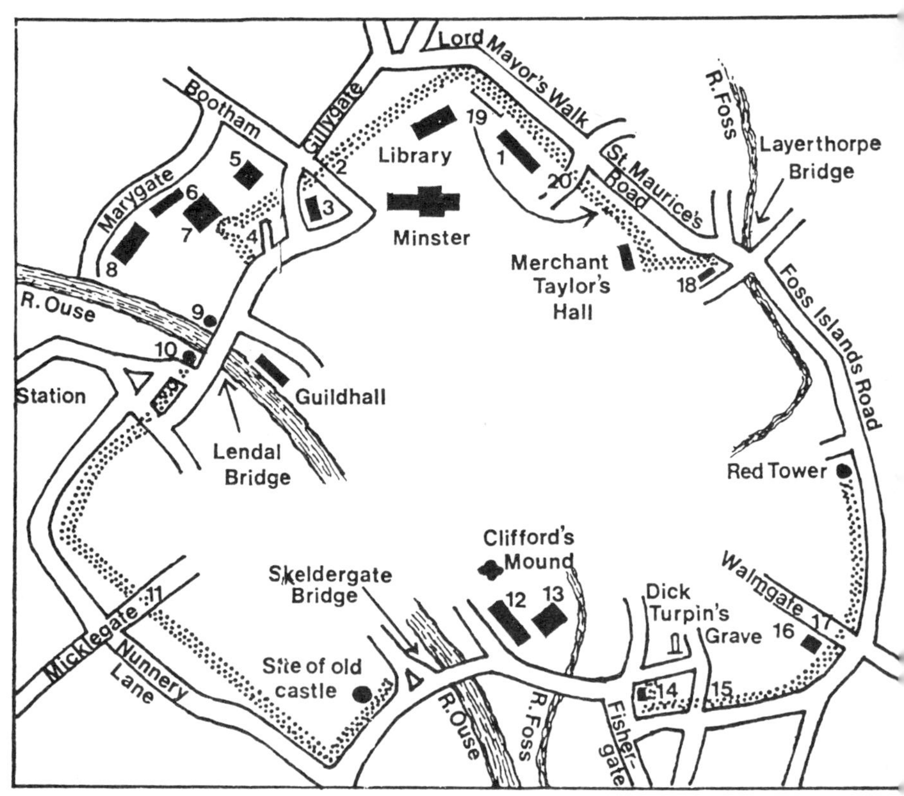

York from the City Walls

KEY TO MAP:

1. Treasurer's House
2. Boothman Bar
3. Theatre Royal
4. Information Office and Library
5. King's Manor
6. St. Mary's Abbey
7. Yorkshire Museum and Gardens
8. St. Olave's Church
9. Lendal Tower
10. Barker Tower
11. Micklegate Bar
12. Assize Courts
13. Castle Museum
14. Fishergate Postern
15. Fishergate Bar
16. Elizabethan house
17. Walmgate Bar
18. St. Cuthbert's Church
19. Roman section of wall
20. Monk Bar

BOOTHAM BAR AND YORK MINSTER.

Knavesmire and the Theatre Royal both opened in the 18th century and continue to be magnets today. York saw a great burst of new building in the 1700s, and a whole school of craftsmen made the city known. Georgians left a pronounced impression on York, particularly in the former town houses along such streets as Micklegate and Bootham. Notable public buildings of the 18th century include the Mansion House, Assembly Rooms, Judge's Lodgings and Assize Courts. The early 18th century Debtors' Prison and the later Female Prison, almost equally grand, now house the justly famous Castle Museum with its period rooms and streets. The Mansion House is the official residence of the Lord Mayor, but can be seen (along with its exceptionally large collection of civic plate) by arrangement. Just behind it is the 15th century Guildhall, bombed in 1942 but restored in 1960. At Bishopthorpe, 2½ miles south of York, is the Archbishop's Palace, which includes traces of an Early English structure. Excursion boats from York's Lendal Bridge take visitors past the Palace on the River Ouse. The fine church opposite was built in 1799 and replaced the old church, the remains of which are reached by taking the lane alongside the Palace to the riverside. This corner is well worth a look at; the beautiful west front still stands and a cross commemorates the site of the High Altar.

Bolton Percy

The church here dates back to 1411, although there are traces of a Norman structure. The present font was consecrated on July 8, 1424. The east window represents five Saint Archbishops: Paulinus, Chad, Wilfrid, John of Beverley and William. The Arms are of Bishops Scrupe, Bowitt, Kem, Booth and Neville. The present altar is a combination of three. In the oak stalls at the west end of the chancel, notice mutilation said to have been caused by the Parliamentarian soldiers when re-sharpening their swords.

Bolton Percy has one of the small number of surviving timber-framed gatehouses in England. In the Middle Ages many large houses were situated in an enclosure entered through a gatehouse, but few such buildings have survived. The Bolton Percy Gatehouse was the entrance to the courtyard of the medieval rectory. It was built in 1467 by Thomas Pearson; a yeoman's son, he made his fortune through successively holding the offices of commissary to the chancellor of the University of Oxford, commissary to the

BOLTON PERCY GATEHOUSE.

archdeacon of Richmond and sub-dean of York, dying a comparatively wealthy man. He was thus well able to afford to build an impressive gatehouse to the courtyard of his rectory, which was itself an impressive building, fitted with stained glass and tapestries. The courtyard also contained a large timber-framed tithe barn and, in the post-medieval period, a dovecot, stables and other farm buildings. The medieval rectory was rebuilt in 1698 and the out-buildings, with the exception of the gatehouse, were all demolished in the first half of the nineteenth century, when the farmyard was turned into a garden.

The moulded tiebeams and carved knee-braces in the principal chamber of the upper floor of the gatehouse show that it had some use additional to its providing an entrance-way to the rectory courtyard, as this impressive room was obviously intended to be seen from the inside, and not just used as a granary, as it was in the eighteenth century. It is possible that it acted as a meeting room for vestry meetings or for a religious guild.

The walls of the gatehouse are close-studded, which was the most expensive form of timber framing, the studs more closely spaced on the south-eastern, outer side than the other. The roof has trusses with short principals and both a collar purlin and side purlins, and is in form related to roofs constructed in the period 1450-1550 in York and Lincoln. The first floor was jettied on all sides, the north-eastern end being supported on dragon posts.

The gatehouse is notable for its carved decoration. The dragon posts are carved with a lion's head, the head of a man with two tongues, two heads in one wimple and an acanthus leaf. The end of each joist was originally decorated with a nailed-on plaque. Only three of these survive; two on the south-eastern side of the building represent a king's head and an acantus leaf, and that on the north-western side is carved with a head of a green man, a medieval fertility figure. The stone footings of the gatehouse, on which can be seen a number of masons' marks, incorporate a large stone coffin and a fragment of a coffin lid. Other fragments of stonework, dating from the twelfth century to the post-medieval period, can be seen built into the walls of the gatehouse courtyard. These may have come from the medieval rectory, an earlier church or Bolton Percy Castle, whose site is lost.

(Details kindly provided by Bolton Percy Gatehouse Restoration Fund, Farnley Hall, Farnley Park, Leeds)

Appleton Roebuck

Two miles north-west of Bolton Percy is the scattered village of Appleton Roebuck. Here are several quaint cottages, built on strong timber frames which will be found most interesting. Just on the outskirts of Appleton by the side of the lane leading to Acaster Selby is a meadow, called by the village children "The Daffy Field" after the daffodils that grow there.

Conclusion

I HOPE you have enjoyed the walk and all the interesting places which I do assure you are very well worth looking at if you can get the time.

I thank everyone again for all the help and all the information that has gone into producing this book. Please keep to the Country Code and help the farmers help us to keep the paths and bridleways open. Also, most of all, when you go through any, gates, please shut them behind you so that the animals do not stray onto the roads and tracks, and do not damage crops.

I would like to thank my wife for typing the book. Thank you.

S. Townson.

Books for Walkers

Bilsdale Circuit	*Malcolm Boyes*
Cal-der-Went Walk	*Geoffrey Carr*
Countryside Walks around Bradford	*Senior Wayfarers*
Countryside Walks around Leeds	*Ivan E. Broadhead*
Countryside Walks around Scarborough	*Malcolm Boyes*
Countryside Walks around York	*Ken Piggin*
Crosses Walk	*Malcolm Boyes*
Dales Traverse	*Simon Townson*
The Derwent Way	*Richard C. Kenchington*
Ebor Way	*J. K. E. Piggin*
Eskdale Way	*Louis S. Dale*
Long Distance Walks—	
1. North York Moors and Wolds	*Tony Wimbush*
2. Yorkshire Dales	*Tony Wimbush & Allan Gott*
3. The Peak	*Tony Wimbush*
Lyke Wake Walk	*Bill Cowley*
Nidderdale Way	*J. K. E. Piggin*
Pennine Way	*Kenneth Oldham*
Six Dales Hike	*J. D. Burland*
Trans-Pennine Walk	*Richard Mackrory*
Walking in Bronte Country	*Ramblers' Association*
Walking in Craven Dales	*Colin Speakman*
Walking in Northern Dales	*Ramblers' Association*
Walking in the South Pennines	*Clifford Thompson*
Walking in Teesdale	*Keith Watson*
Walking in the Three Peaks	*Colin Speakman*
Walks From Your Car—	
Bilsdale and the Hambletons	*Ramblers' Association*
Eskdale and the Cleveland Coast	*Ramblers' Association*
Rosedale and Farndale	*Malcolm Boyes*
Walks in Lower Wharfedale	*Geoffrey White*
Walks in Nidderdale	*Geoffrey White*
Walks in Swaledale	*Geoffrey White*
Walks in Upper Wharfedale	*Michael Obst*
Walks in Wensleydale	*Geoffrey White*
Walks North of York	*Geoffrey White & Geoffrey Green*
Walks on the North York Moors	*Ramblers' Association*
Wayfarer Walks in the South Pennines	*Colin Speakman*
White Rose Walk	*Geoffrey White*
Wolds Way	*David Rubinstein*
Yoredale Way	*J. K. E. Piggin*

Send S.A.E. for current book list to Dalesman Books, Clapham, via Lancaster, LA2 8EB.